## KIDS GET LEARNING

Copyright © 2016 by Tyler David. All rights reserved.

No part of these pages, either text or image may be used for any purpose other than personal use. Therefore, reproduction, modification, storage in a retrieval system or retransmission, in any form or by any means, electronic, mechanical or otherwise, for reasons other than personal use, is strictly prohibited without prior written permission.

First published 2017 by 831 Designs

### AfricanImpact
EXPLORE · INSPIRE · IMPACT

Tyler is passionate about helping save Rhinos and Elephants so 10% of his profits he donates to this ENDANGERED BLACK RHINO & ELEPHANT CONSERVATION.

# Foreword

A year ago, I would not be in a position to write this. However, 7 months ago Forever Family Forever Free came into my life. Upon learning of their pain, struggles and more importantly, their successes, it came as no surprise when I learned the incredible things their young children were doing.

This amazing family helped me publish my first book and we're vital in it becoming an *Amazon #1 Best Seller,* as well as *Amazon International Best Seller.* All of this being done while one of their children Tegan was publishing her third book and doing speaking engagements. That in and of itself speaks volumes. But it hasn't stopped there.

Welcome Tyler, their young boy. But unlike most boys his age, heck, unlike most adults, Tyler is quite established. It is not everyday you meet an inventor, but it is even more rare when you meet an inventor under the age of five. And to add to this young enigma's list of accomplishments in now his second book of his series. To write a book is a lifelong goal of so many people in this world and here you have a young boy taking life by the horns and creating the opportunity so many of us fear.

As a Fitness and Transformational Coach I am blown away with his topic for this book. Tyler chose exercise to write about. Exercise, health and wellness is more important than ever. As we evolve and technology advances, there are much more shiny and time consuming activities for youngsters than ever before. Xbox, ipads and the gaming industry in general occupy a vast majority of time for today's youth. According to studies, in the US one-fifth of children are being classified as obese. Regular exercise is not only a great release, but has been proven to reduce the risks for many disease and illnesses such as heart disease, type 2 diabetes, and high blood pressure to name a few.

The importance of this topic for adults is high, but I feel it is even higher for children. Life long habits can be developed in and throughout childhood, so the importance of developing good, healthy, positive habits can play a huge factor in a young person's life. It brings joy to me to write this forward about a topic few are discussing with their children.

Tyler has achieved more in his short five years on this planet than the majority will in a lifetime. His intelligence, fearlessness, flair for life, along with his creative ability have made him a force to be reckon with, now and in the future. Tyler is certainly headed onward and upward. Cheers.

**Matthew A Cybulski No1 International Bestselling Author and Coach - 2017**

# 3 Tips for Aliens

## How to KEEP your Pet Humans HEALTHY

Written By Tyler David

# Step 1

## To have a happy human you need to let them shoot some hoops.

# Your Human

Your pet needs to move around lots to keep their bodies super healthy.

This Spaceship is hidden on every page for you to find.

Hello. I am Dragon Horn.

Hey! I am Red Horn.

Hi. I am Yellow Horn.

The One Horn Brothers

# Meet the team.

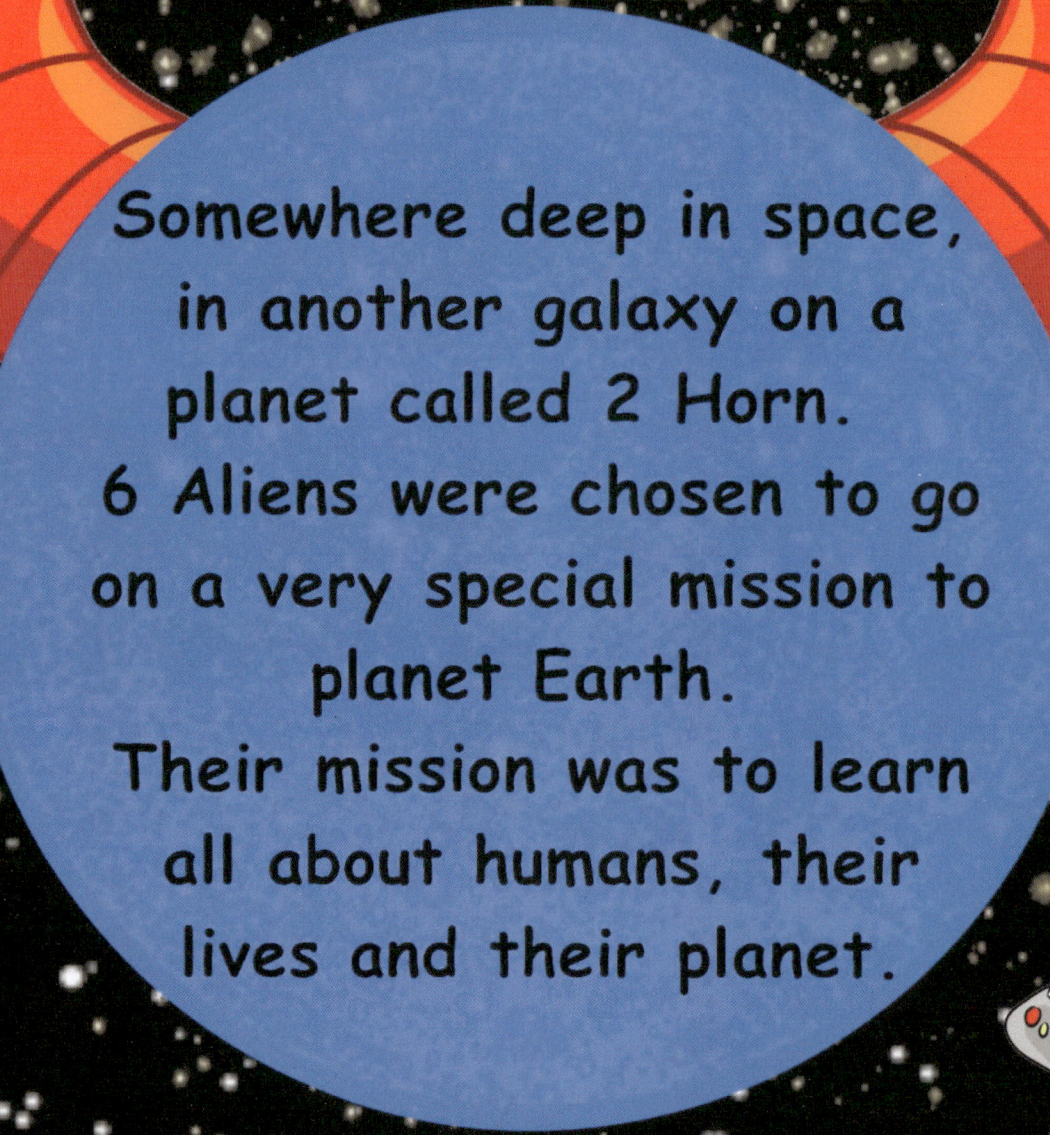

Somewhere deep in space, in another galaxy on a planet called 2 Horn.
6 Aliens were chosen to go on a very special mission to planet Earth.
Their mission was to learn all about humans, their lives and their planet.

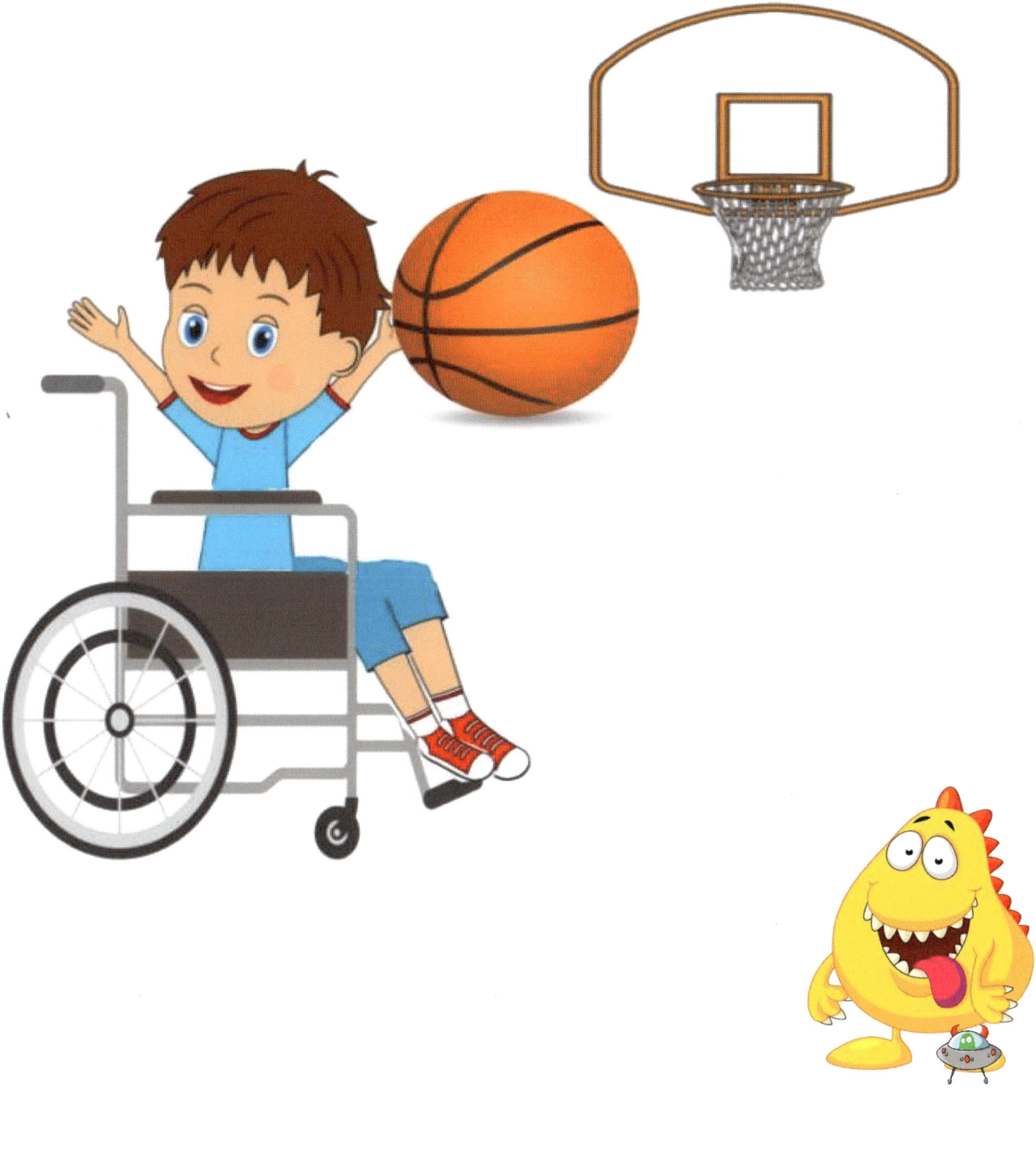

# Do NOT let them stay in all day.

# Step 2

Let your pet Humans jump on their beds!

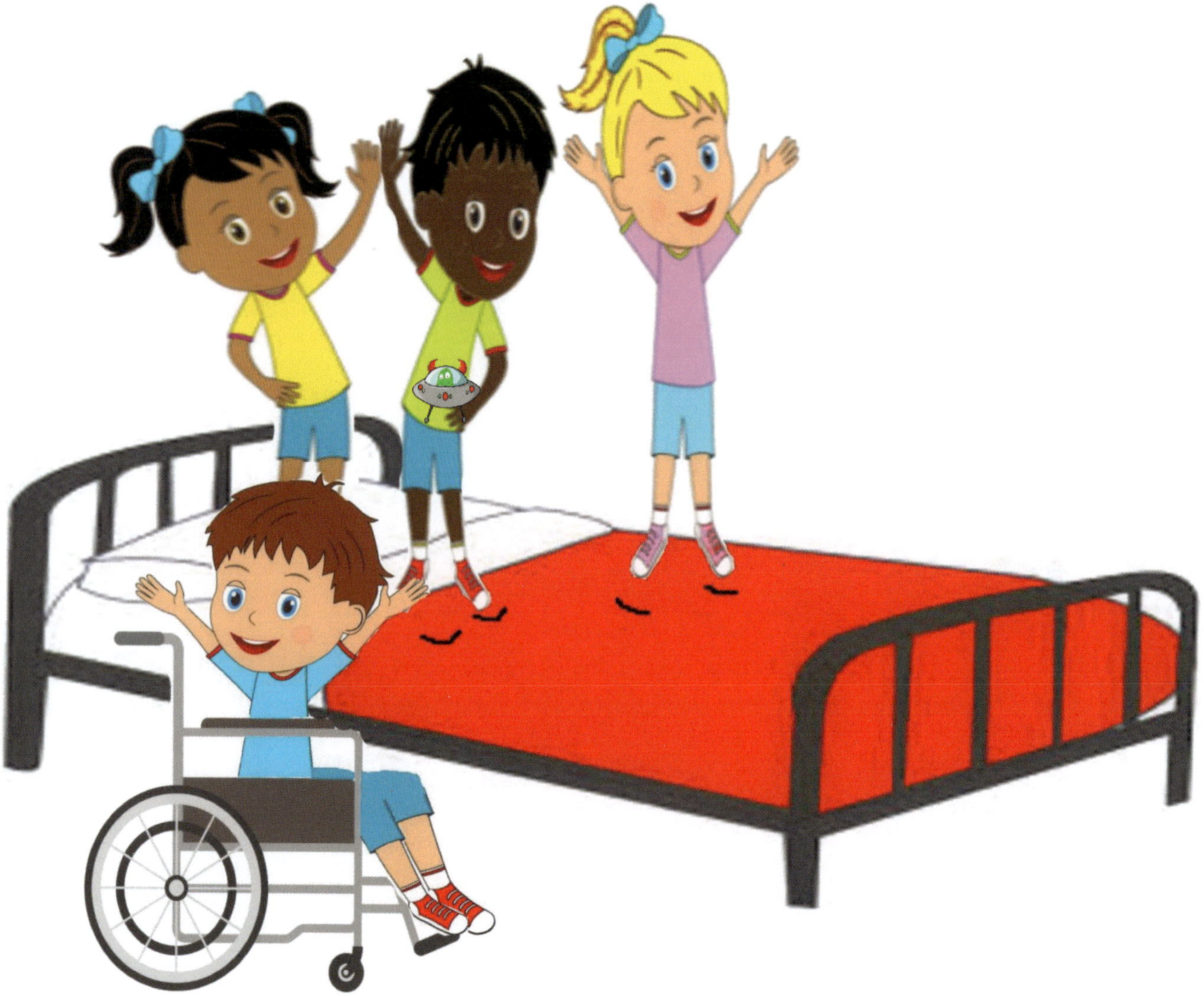

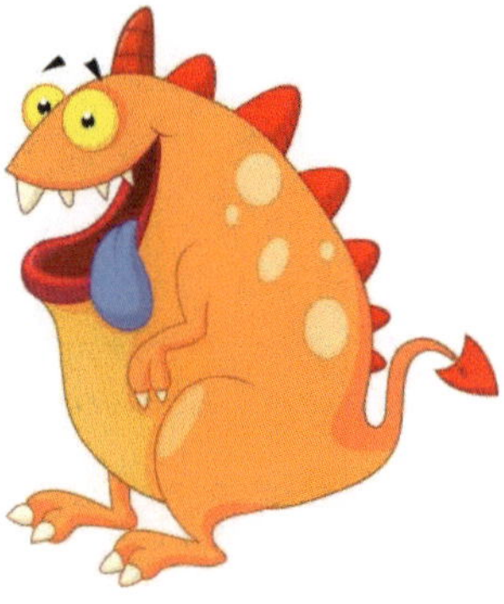

# Do NOT keep them still all day!

# Step 3

Let them play out on their funny wheelie things called bikes.

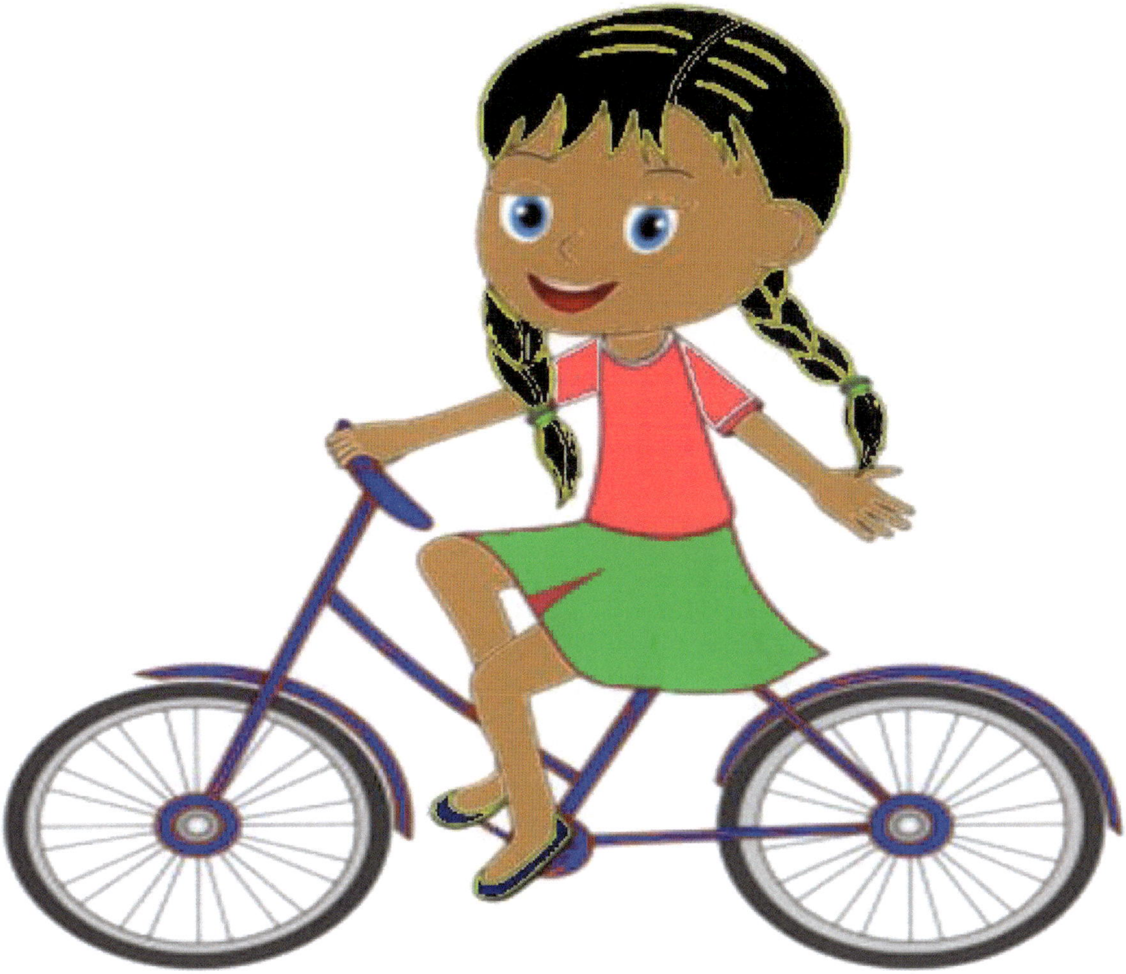
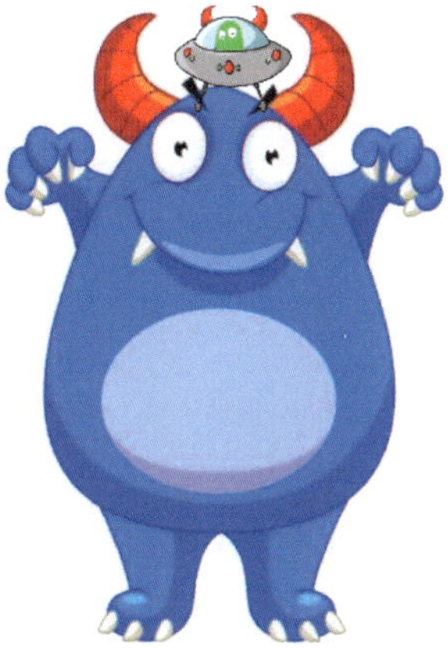

# Do NOT let them get BORED!

Letting your humans Get outdoors and moving their bodies lots, keeps them healthy, happy and strong.

Keeping humans indoors or keeping them still all day, makes them sad, poorly and fat.

Be a great pet owner and take good care of your humans.

# Fun things to do

## Spot the 5 Differences

# What to do today?

# Colour in an alien friend

# Help the human find his basketball?

# Find the words

| r | u | n | n | i | n | g |
|---|---|---|---|---|---|---|
| j | u | m | p | i | n | g |
| n | n | b | a | l | l | t |
| h | o | o | p | s | t | d |
| o | o | n | b | i | k | e |

bike

hoops

ball

jumping

running

If you enjoyed this book please look out for my other books on Amazon

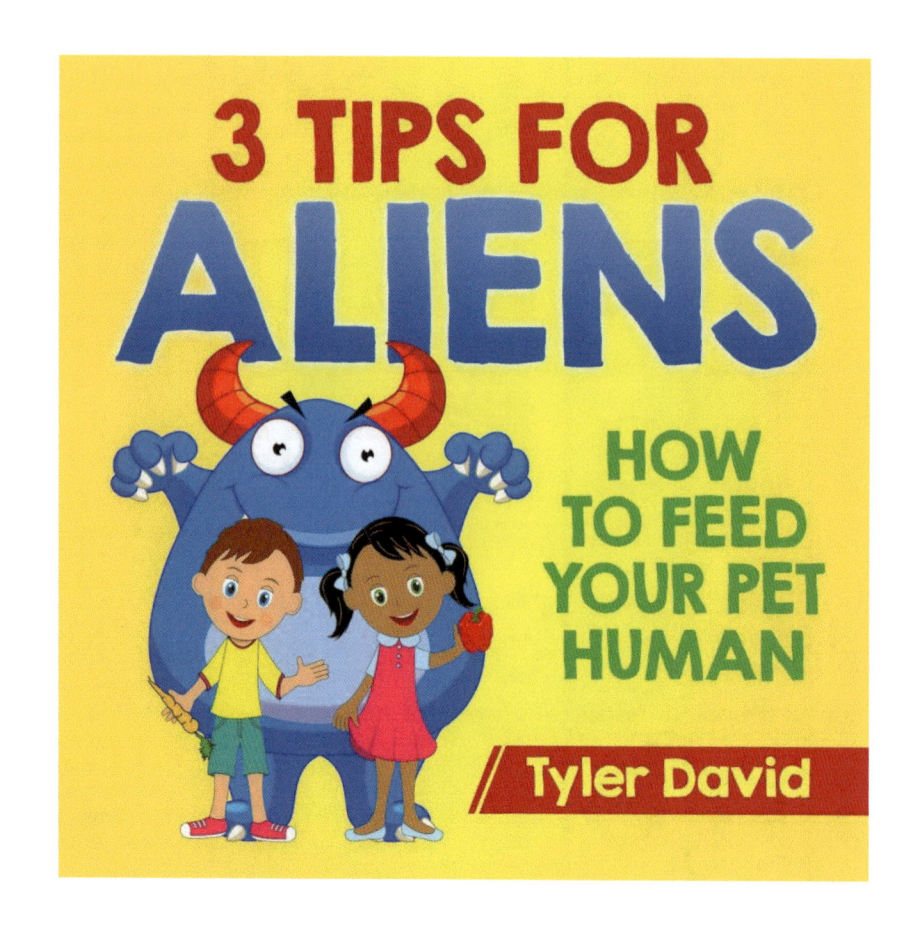

**3 TIPS FOR ALIENS: HOW TO FEED YOUR PET HUMAN** — Tyler David

Thank you for your support I am really grateful.

# More books from Tyler David

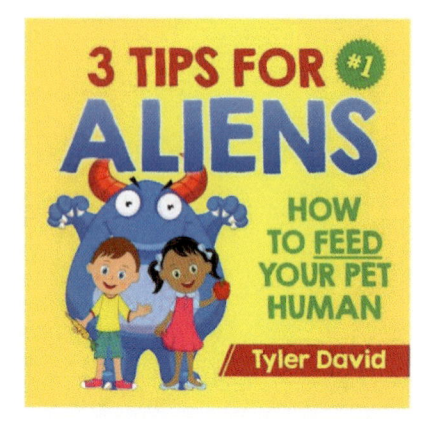

**3 TIPS FOR ALIENS #1 — HOW TO FEED YOUR PET HUMAN**
Tyler David

This book is a great fun way for kids to learn all about healthy eating and drinking, to learn what is good for their bodies. this is suitable for all, vegetarians, vegans, gluten free and other allergies. Using whole foods and organic produce.

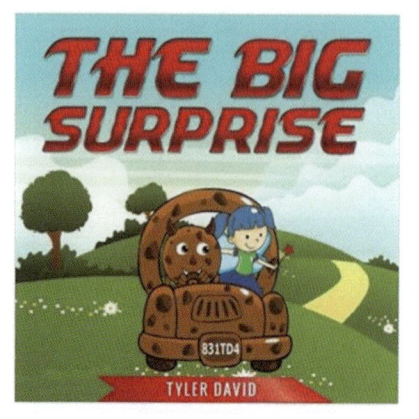

**THE BIG SURPRISE**
Tyler David

Tyler's first ever book! Tyler David the little boy with a huge heart for adventure. Takes you on a fun journey in his first ever book. A super fun read for you and your children to share.

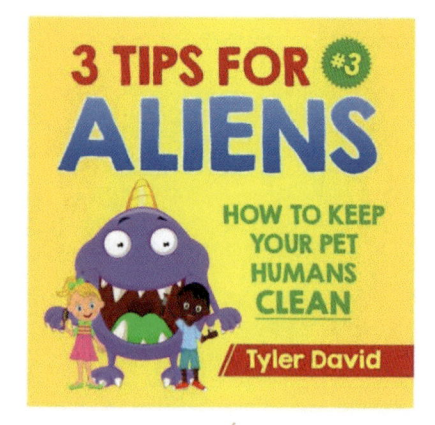

**3 TIPS FOR ALIENS #3 — HOW TO KEEP YOUR PET HUMANS CLEAN**
Tyler David

A fun way for your child to learn about brushing our teeth, hair and keeping clean. Written by a child for children. Tyler (age 5) is passionate about helping kids be healthy and strong, So they have plenty of time to play and be happy. Including fun activities. Third in a series

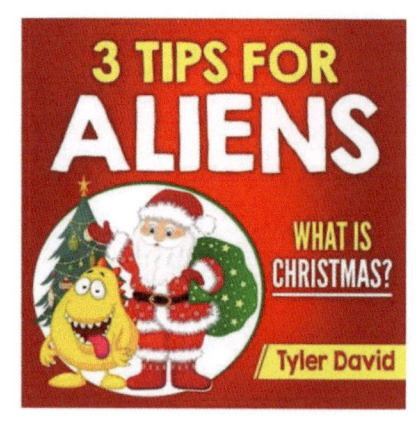

**3 TIPS FOR ALIENS — WHAT IS CHRISTMAS?**
Tyler David

A fun way for your child to learn all about Christmas. Written by a child for children. Tyler (age 5) is passionate about learning all the fun times of year. So kids have plenty of time to plan, play and be happy. Including fun activities. Part of a series

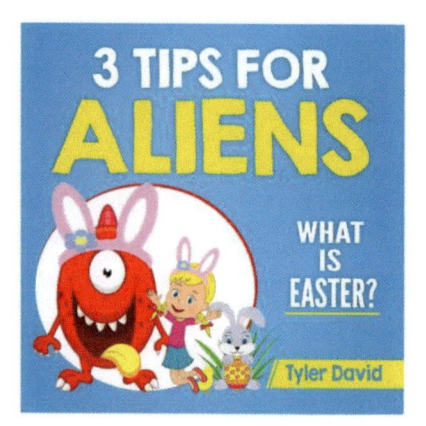

**3 TIPS FOR ALIENS — WHAT IS EASTER?**
Tyler David

A fun way for your child to learn all about Easter.
Written by a child for children. Tyler (age 5) is passionate about learning all the fun times of year. So they have plenty of time to plan, play and be happy. Including fun activities. Part of a series

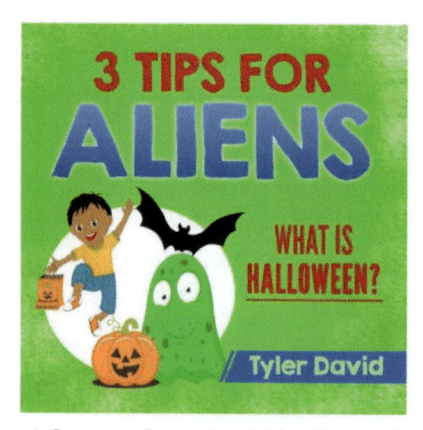

**3 TIPS FOR ALIENS — WHAT IS HALLOWEEN?**
Tyler David

A fun way for your child to learn all about Halloween.
Written by a child for children. Tyler (age 5) is passionate about learning all the fun times of year. So they have plenty of time to plan, play and be happy. Including fun activities. Part of a series

# More books from Forever Family Forever Free

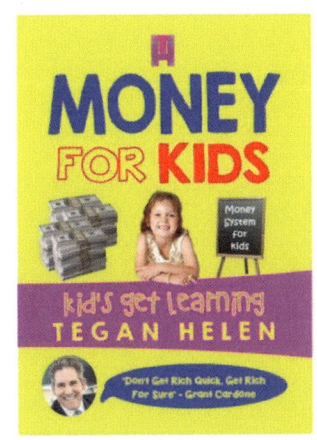

Children really need to have and read this book lots so they never have to get a job and work. Losing your free time for fun things, to having to go work to get money instead. If you learn everything in this book all about money and what to do with it, and really understand it all. You will never need to work for money and your never to have a Job. Money is everywhere and everything. If we can understand it and learn to control it, you will never have to work for money. Let your money work for you so you can enjoy your life doing the things you enjoy doing.

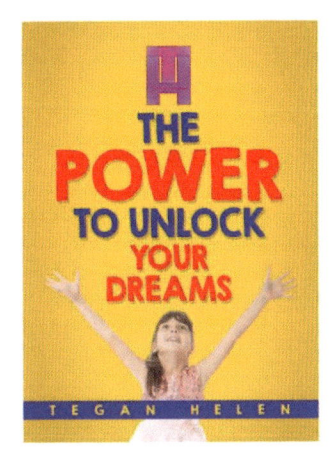

Tegan Helen is a true inspiration, she had a really challenging start in life but was saved at age three, she has such drive, and is so full of Love! She loves to read and write and hopes to help loads of children, reach their dreams and live a life of happiness, she also believes in giving back as a percentage of each book sold goes to charities close to her heart. Her latest book is based on the law of attraction, broken down in a way all kids will get it and can get out there and reach for the stars! A must read for any kid.

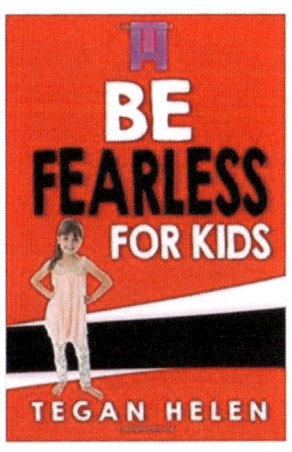

Incredible book third in a series of books for kids who want big changes and big success. Be fearless for kids teaches kids, techniques and useful tools on how to become fearless, in any situation. helps them grow in self confidence, face challenges head on with no fear, and how to stand in their truth. incredible 7 year old author suitable for kids age 4 - 99

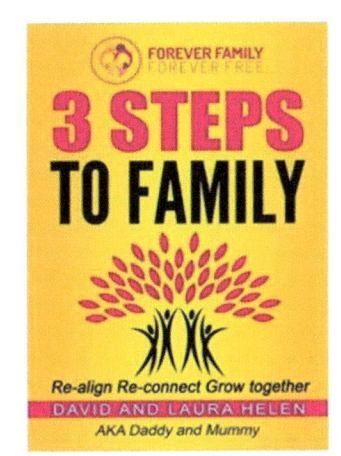

Worlds greatest family share their hearts, passion and success, to teach other families to achieve the same. We help families become stronger, by helping them realign, reconnect and grow together, we do this as a loving family leading the way, the life we live is the proven example.

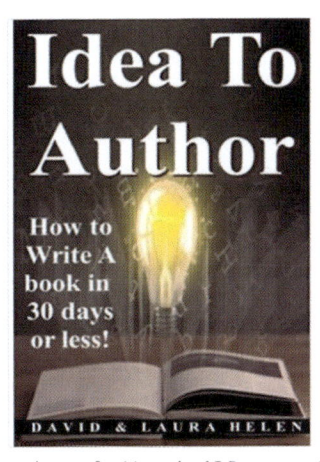

Do you dream of writing a book? Do you want the Authority and Credibility that comes with being a published author? Do you want to do this on a low Budget? This is the easiest Step by Step GUIDE on how to achieve this? David & Laura Helen CEO's of 831 Designs publishers, Have done all the hard work for you, Simplified it and made it so easy a child can do it. If you have a child who like Tyler wants to start creating books, this is this cheapest way to help them to start creating.

**KIDS GET LEARNING**

Printed in Great Britain
by Amazon

12324950R00022